T0419613

# UNSOLVED
# PYRAMIDS OF EGYPT

*DINAH WILLIAMS*

**Children's Press®**

An imprint of Scholastic Inc.

Special thanks to our fact-checker M. L. Liu

Library of Congress Cataloging-in-Publication Data available

ISBN 978-1-5461-4154-9 (library binding) | ISBN 978-1-5461-4155-6 (paperback)

10 9 8 7 6 5 4 3 2 1          25 26 27 28 29

Printed in China 62

First edition, 2025

Book design by Kay Petronio

Photos ©: back cover top: F1online digitale Bildagentur GmbH/Alamy Images; 3: Anton Aleksenko/Getty Images; 4: Islam Moawad/Getty Images; 5: Jim McMahon/Mapman ®; 6–7: CHINE NOUVELLE/SIPA/Shutterstock; 8: Foxie_aka_Ashes/Getty Images; 9: HALED ELFIQI/EPA-EFE/Shutterstock; 10–11: DEA PICTURE LIBRARY/De Agostini/Getty Images; 13: Budget Direct; 14: Look and Learn/Peter Jackson Collection/Bridgeman Images; 15: Look and Learn/Bridgeman Images; 16: Will & Deni McIntyre/Getty Images; 17: Giorgio Albertini. All Rights Reserved 2024/Bridgeman Images; 18–19: Ancient Art and Architecture Collection Ltd./Bridgeman Images; 20: Q-Files, Ltd.; 21, 22–23 : Jean-Claude Golvin; 24: Penta Springs Limited/Alamy Images; 26–27: RaRa/Alamy Images; 28: Patrick Landmann/Getty Images; 29: Art Media/Print Collector/Getty Images; 31: Dorling Kindersley/Getty Images; 32: Islam Moawad/Getty Images; 36: Shutterstock; 37: jarino47/Getty Images; 38: Ben Curtis/AP Images; 39: Look and Learn/Bridgeman Images; 40: Giza Project/Harvard University; 41 top: The Egyptian Ministry of Antiquities; 41 bottom: Ahmed Gomaa/Xinhua/Getty Images; 44 top left: Anton Petrus/Getty Images; 44 top right: F1online digitale Bildagentur GmbH/Alamy Images; 44 bottom left: Goddard_Photography/Getty Images; 44 bottom right: Givaga/Getty Images; 45 top right: Stefano Bianchetti/Bridgeman Images; 45 bottom left: Look and Learn/Bridgeman Images; 45 bottom right: The Egyptian Ministry of Antiquities; 46 top left: diegograndi/Getty Images; 46 bottom left: Alfredo Estrella/AFP/Getty Images.

All other photos © Shutterstock.

# CONTENTS

# AN ANCIENT MYSTERY

Great Pyramid

The pyramids of Egypt have amazed people for centuries. The largest pyramids are in the city of Giza. They are considered engineering marvels. The tallest one is called the Great Pyramid. It was 481 feet (147 m) tall. That is nearly forty stories high! It was the tallest building in the world for over 3,500 years.

Egypt is a country in Africa. Today, Giza is Egypt's third largest city. The Nile River runs to the east of Giza.

## MAP OF EGYPT

Mediterranean Sea

Alexandria

Cairo

Giza

SINAI PENINSULA

Area of map

ASIA

AFRICA

SAUDI ARABIA

EGYPT

LIBYA

Nile

Red Sea

Luxor

**North**
NW — NE
**West** — **East**
SW — SE
**South**

**KEY**
⭐ Capital city
● City
🔺 Great Pyramid

Lake Nasser

SUDAN

About 14 million tourists visit the pyramids of Giza each year.

The Great Pyramid is one of the Seven Wonders of the Ancient World.

We know thousands of workers built the pyramids. But we still don't know exactly how they did it. We know they used millions of giant stones. Some came from miles away. But how did the **ancient** Egyptians move them?

Wheels had not been invented yet. How were the stones cut to size and lifted? The tools we use today did not exist at the time, either. Researchers have different **theories**. Let's explore this mystery!

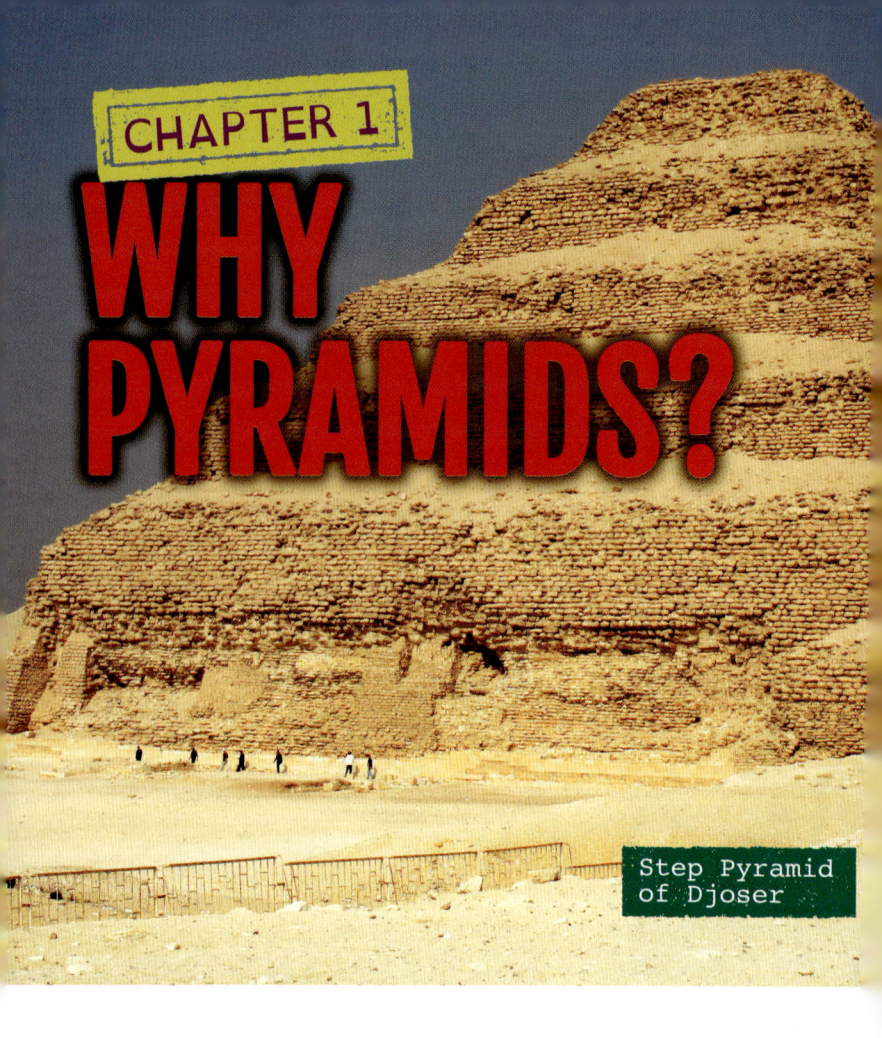

# CHAPTER 1

# WHY PYRAMIDS?

Step Pyramid of Djoser

The pyramids were built to house the body of the king when he died. The king in ancient Egypt was called a pharaoh. After death, a pharaoh was thought to be a god. So, his **tomb** had to be impressive.

8

The first pyramid was completed by the pharaoh Djoser in 2630 **BCE**. It was 200 feet (61 m) tall. The outside looked like steps. The inside had rooms. Some were decorated to look like a palace.

Djoser's pyramid was restored. This is one of the tunnels.

Egyptians believed in life after death. They thought a person's spirit passed on to the land of the dead. This was called the **afterlife**. Egyptians also believed the body had to be **preserved**. This would allow the spirit to travel between life and death.

The Egyptians built tombs inside the pyramids. Pharaohs were buried inside the tombs. The tombs had everything the pharaoh would need in the afterlife. This included food and tools. The tombs were often also filled with treasures.

This is a model of a pharaoh's tomb. It is filled with treasures.

11

Khufu became pharaoh around 2550 BCE. He viewed himself as a god. His tomb had to be better than the tombs built before him.

Khufu also wanted a pyramid for his tomb. The shape was thought to help the pharaoh's spirit reach the afterlife. So, Khufu decided to build the biggest pyramid ever. It is called the Great Pyramid.

The only known statue of Khufu is 3 inches (7.6 cm) tall. It was found in 1903.

# WHITE PYRAMIDS?

The pyramids were built using **limestone**. Limestone is a hard rock used in building. Tan limestone blocks were placed down first. They were covered in shiny, white limestone. Researchers believe the top point was covered in gold.

The Great Pyramid probably used to look like this.

Egyptian workers moving giant blocks of limestone.

Khufu chose the valley in Giza for his pyramid. No other pharaohs were buried there. There was limestone in nearby cliffs.

Men came from all over Egypt to work on the Great Pyramid. Some might have been farmers. Once a year, the Nile flooded. This meant they could not work on their land. It is believed there were as many as 20,000 workers! But nobody knows for sure.

Building the Great Pyramid might have looked like this.

15

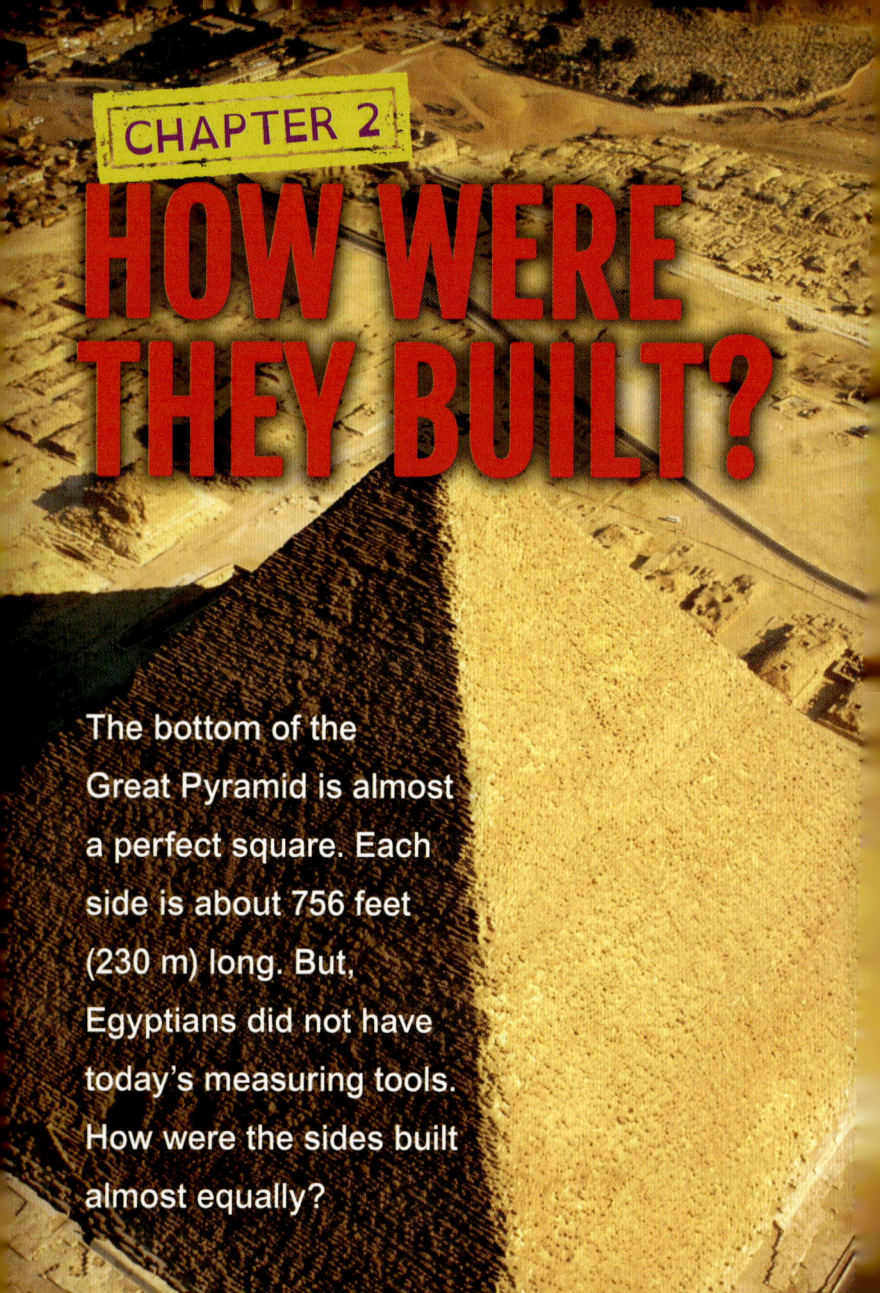

# CHAPTER 2

# HOW WERE THEY BUILT?

The bottom of the Great Pyramid is almost a perfect square. Each side is about 756 feet (230 m) long. But, Egyptians did not have today's measuring tools. How were the sides built almost equally?

16

Tan-colored limestone blocks were used. Each weighed two and a half tons. They used 2.3 million blocks to build the pyramid. Granite was used to build the pharaoh's tomb inside the pyramid. One block weighed up to 80 tons! How were the workers able to cut the stones?

## CUTOUT OF THE GREAT PYRAMID

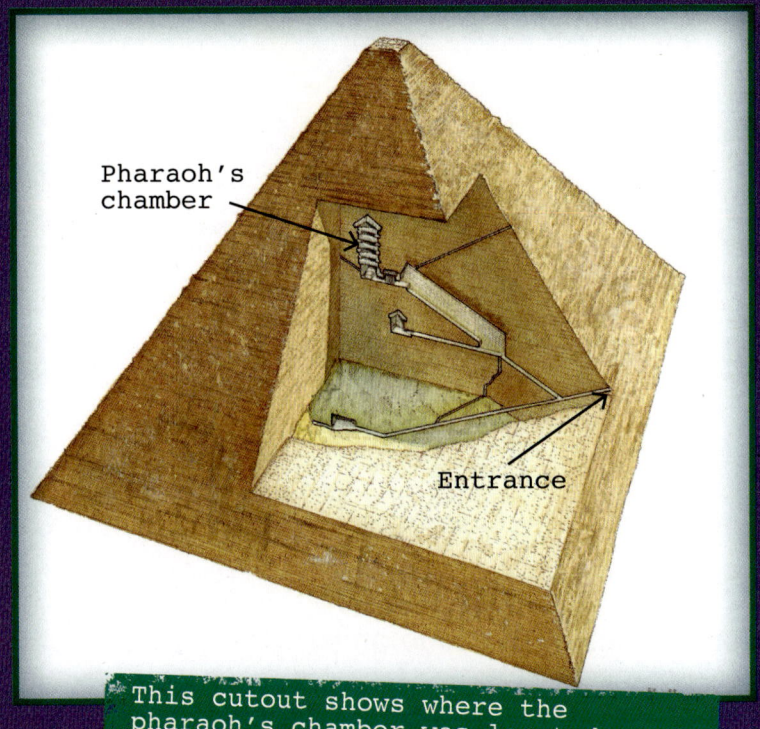

Pharaoh's chamber

Entrance

This cutout shows where the pharaoh's chamber was located. Khufu's tomb is inside the chamber.

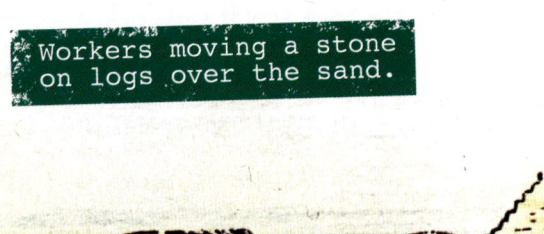
Workers moving a stone on logs over the sand.

How did the Egyptians move the stones without wheels? There are many theories. Maybe the workers rolled the stone on logs over the sand.

Maybe the workers wet the sand to help slide the stones. Or maybe they used wet desert clay instead. But the giant stones would still be difficult to move.

It is possible the Nile River used to run closer to Giza. Researchers have found writing from a man named Merer. He was alive when the pyramids were built. He wrote about working with his men. They brought limestone up the Nile to Giza.

There might have been a harbor close to Giza.

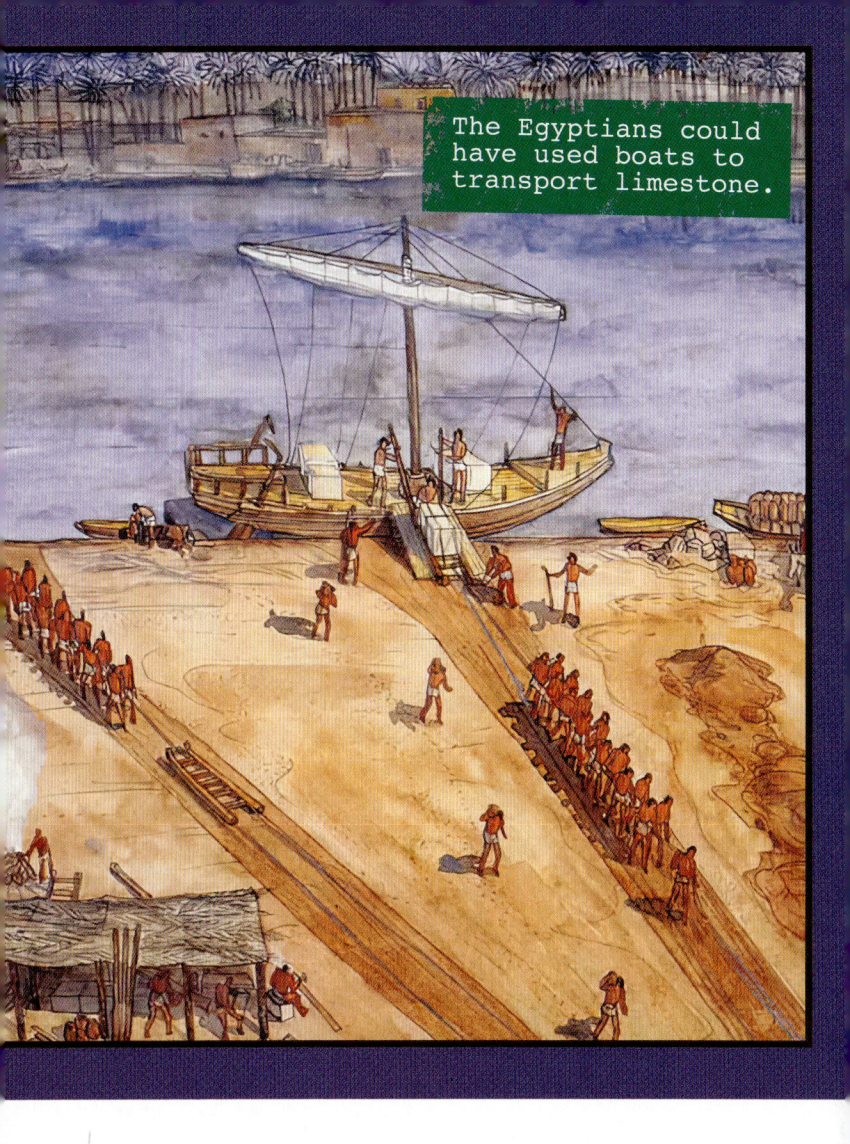

The Egyptians could have used boats to transport limestone.

Researchers drilled holes into the ground near the pyramids. Evidence of a river was found. So, the massive stones could have been floated to Giza.

This drawing shows Egyptian workers using levers.

How did the workers move the stones up the sides of the pyramid? No one knows for sure. **Pulleys** had not been invented yet. Maybe a ramp was built around the pyramid.

Workers then used **levers** to raise the stones higher. But the ramp would have to be as big as the pyramid. What happened to the ramp after it was used? No evidence of it has been found.

Some of the stone blocks were cut almost perfectly. Each block was placed carefully. There is barely room for a knife blade between the blocks. It's a mystery how workers fit the blocks together. Maybe the Egyptians used copper chisels to cut the stones. However, none have ever been found in Giza.

This copper chisel was discovered in a different part of Egypt.

You can see how tightly the stone blocks were placed.

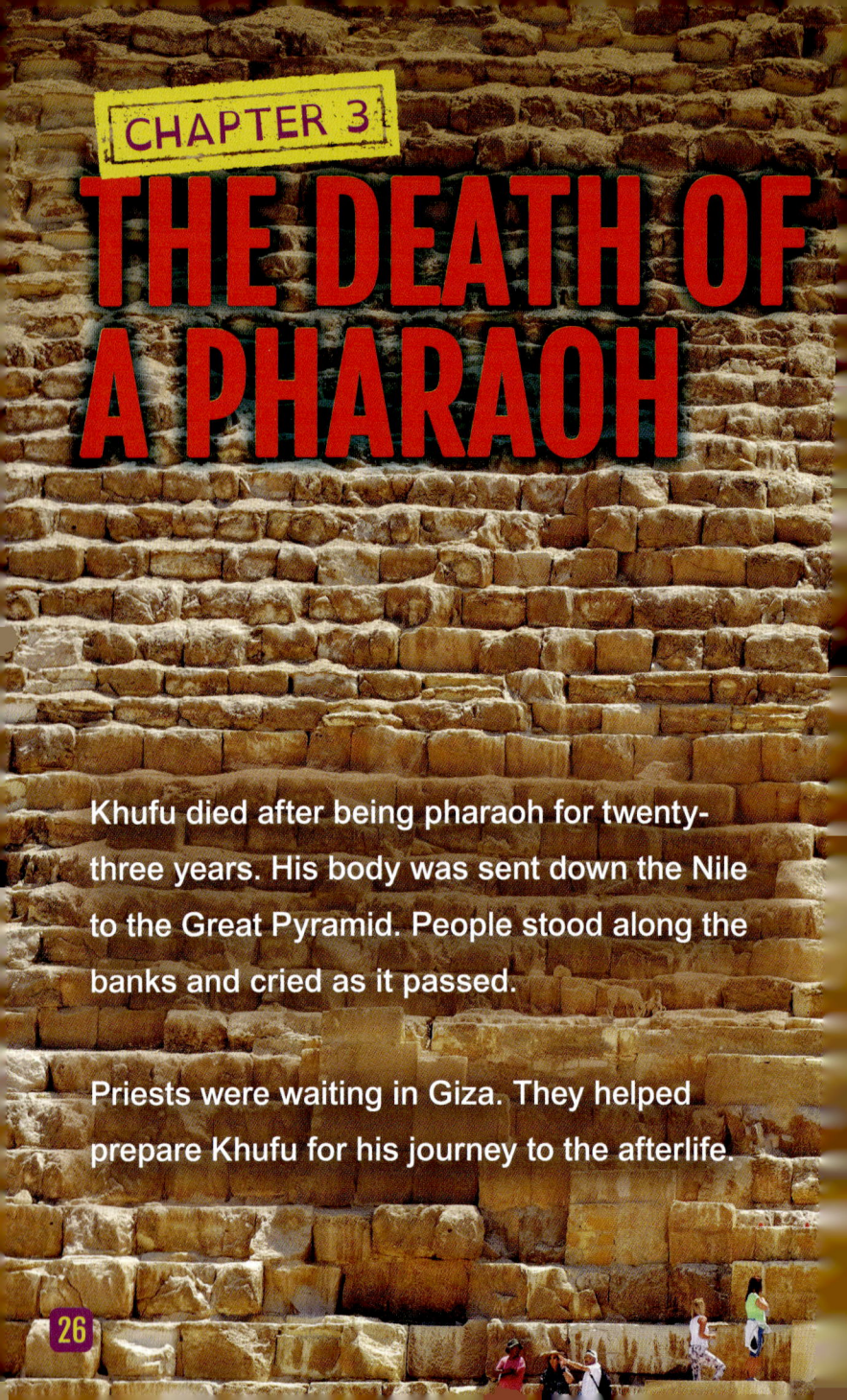

# CHAPTER 3
# THE DEATH OF A PHARAOH

Khufu died after being pharaoh for twenty-three years. His body was sent down the Nile to the Great Pyramid. People stood along the banks and cried as it passed.

Priests were waiting in Giza. They helped prepare Khufu for his journey to the afterlife.

This hole is the entrance to Khufu's Great Pyramid.

Egyptians believed the spirit needed a body after death. They made the body into a **mummy** to make it last. The organs were taken out and put in jars. The body was filled with salt for a time. This helped dry it out. Jewels and gold decorated the body. It was then wrapped in cloth and put into a wood coffin.

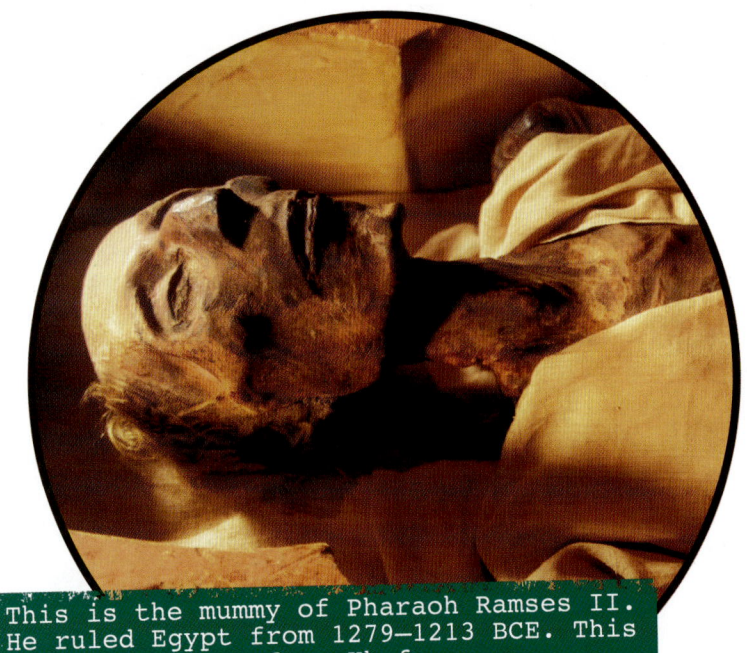

This is the mummy of Pharaoh Ramses II. He ruled Egypt from 1279—1213 BCE. This was many years after Khufu.

The cover of this Egyptian coffin is on the right. The wrapped mummy inside is on the left.

The process took seventy days. Khufu was then buried in his tomb in the center of the pyramid. The entrance was sealed.

Khafre's pyramid (middle) looks taller because it was built on higher ground. Khufu's pyramid (back) is the tallest in height.

Khufu's son Khafre became pharaoh. He, too, wanted a pyramid for the afterlife. Thousands of workers began building again in Giza. Khafre's son also built a pyramid there. His name was Menkaure.

The mummies of Khafre and Menkaure were also buried inside their pyramids.

# CHANGES OVER TIME

What happened to the white limestone on the outside of the pyramids? Researchers believe it cracked over time. It was then taken to construct other buildings. That is why the pyramids are tan, not white. They are also shorter than before. The Great Pyramid now measures about 450 ft (137 m) tall. That's 31 ft (9 m) shorter!

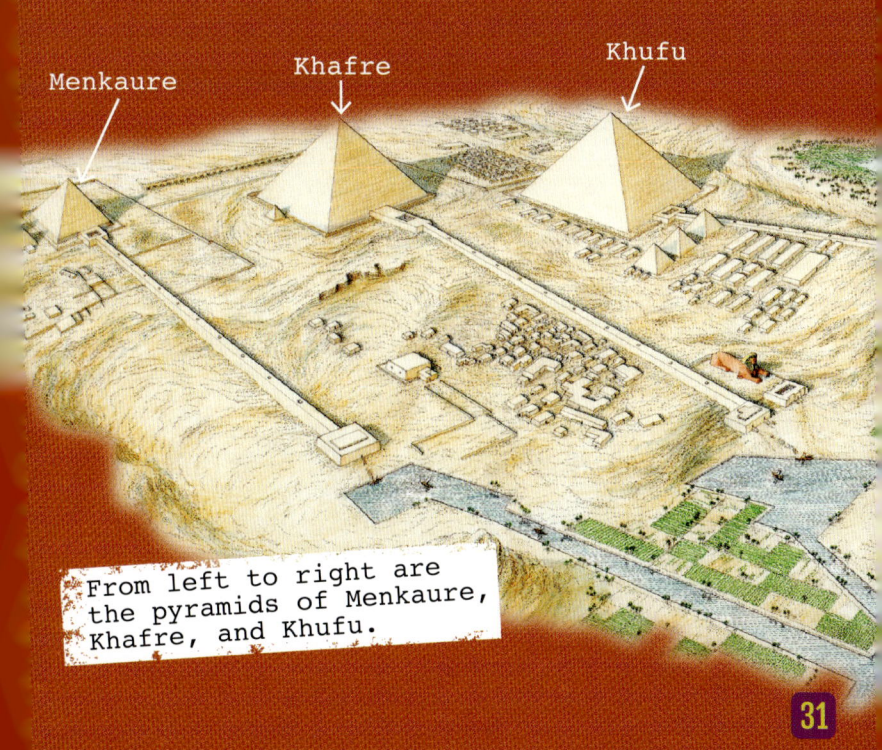

Menkaure

Khafre

Khufu

From left to right are the pyramids of Menkaure, Khafre, and Khufu.

Builders probably used the sun's path to place the pyramids.

Some believe the Egyptians had help building the pyramids. They are too amazing to have been built by men at the time. Could aliens have helped?

The Great Pyramid has four sides. They are facing exactly north, south, east, and west. But they were built before the compass was invented. The pyramids might have pointed to stars in the sky. Egyptians believed the gods of the afterlife lived in these stars. But you could only see the stars lining up from above. Some believe this is evidence of alien assistance.

Today, the stars in the night sky are not in the same place. They have moved since the pyramids were built.

South of the Great Pyramid is the Great Sphinx.
Its construction is also a mystery. At 66 feet (20 m)
high, it is one of the world's largest sculptures.
It has the face of a man and the body of a lion.
When was it built? No one knows for sure.

The Great Sphinx was carved from one enormous piece of limestone.

The face could be either Khufu or Khafre. It probably took one hundred workers three years to carve the statue. It may have also been painted at one time. There is a small **temple** in front of its paws.

King Tutankhamun's tomb was discovered 400 miles (644 km) south of Giza.

Other pharaohs had tombs built across Egypt. They were filled with treasures. But over time, grave robbers stole from them. They even took the pharaohs' mummies for their jewels and gold.

Only one pharaoh's tomb has been found mostly untouched. Tutankhamun was a pharaoh from 1333–1324 BCE. His tomb was discovered underground by Howard Carter in 1922. The nineteen-year-old king was buried with amazing riches. His gold coffin was estimated to be worth at least one million US dollars in today's money.

King Tutankhamun's gold coffin was a famous discovery!

Many Egyptian tombs had curses carved on their entrances. They were put there to prevent robbers from stealing. The pharaoh's spirit would haunt anyone who disturbed their tomb.

This is a curse inscribed into a doorway to an Egyptian tomb. It warns thieves they will be eaten by crocodiles and snakes.

This drawing shows the discovery of Menkaure's tomb.

Explorer R. W. Howard Vyse searched the pyramids. He discovered Menkaure's **sarcophagus** in 1837. It was supposed to be sent to England. But the ship sank mysteriously into the sea. It has never been found. Could the curses be true?

39

# CHAPTER 4

# WHAT TO BELIEVE?

This is a digital 3D model of the pyramids.

Researchers have studied the pyramids of Giza for centuries. They are still trying to determine how they were built. Some constructed models. Some tested out theories. In 2023, a hidden hallway was discovered in the Great Pyramid. In 2024, a new theory was suggested. Water might have been used to lift stones inside the Step Pyramid. Who knows what might be discovered next!

An image of the Great Pyramid's hidden hallway (top). Inside the center of the Step Pyramid of Djoser (bottom).

So how were the Egyptian pyramids built? People are still trying to solve the mystery. We haven't found any pharaoh's records. They probably wanted people to be amazed. The pyramids were a way to show the world their power.

This mystery may remain unsolved. What do you believe? Maybe you're not sure. Maybe we'll never know how these amazing structures were built!

It is common to see camels near the pyramids.

43

# TIMELINE: Then and Now

**Djoser built the Step Pyramid.**

**The Pyramid of Khafre is completed.**

| 2630 BCE | 2560 BCE | 2530 BCE | 2530 BC (estimate) |

**The Great Pyramid of of Khufu is completed.**

**The Great Sphin is completed.**

**The Pyramid of Menkaure is completed.**

**Howard Carter discovers Tutankhamun's tomb.**

| 510 BCE | 1837 | 1922 | 2023 |

**R. W. Howard Vyse finds Menkaure's sarcophagus.**

**A hidden hallway is discovered in the Great Pyramid.**

# PYRAMIDS AROUND THE WORLD

There were other pyramids built in North and Central America. Ancient people used them to worship their gods. Some buried their kings in them, too. Here are a few examples!

Great Pyramid of Cholula
Puebla, Mexico

Temple IV
Tikal, Guatemala

Pyramid of the Sun
Teotihuacán, Mexico

El Castillo
Chichén Itzá, Mexico

# GLOSSARY

**afterlife** (AF-tur-life) an existence after death

**ancient** (AYN-shuhnt) belonging to a period long ago

**BCE** "Before the Common Era," used to refer to the years before the birth of Jesus Christ

**lever** (LEV-ur) a bar resting on a turning point, used to lift an object placed on one end by pushing down on the other end

**limestone** (LIME-stohn) a hard rock used in building and in making lime and cement

**mummy** (MUHM-ee) a dead body that has been preserved with special chemicals and wrapped in cloth

**preserve** (pri-ZURV) to protect something so that it stays in its original or current state

**pulley** (PUL-ee) a lifting machine made from a rope or chain

**sarcophagus** (sar-KAH-fuh-guhs) a stone coffin

**Seven Wonders of the Ancient World** seven famous, human-made structures built during BCE that travelers wanted to visit

**temple** (TEM-puhl) a building used for worshipping a god or gods

**theory** (THEER-ee) an idea or statement that explains how or why something happens

**tomb** (toom) a grave, room, or building for holding a dead body

# INDEX

## ABOUT THE AUTHOR

Dinah Williams, who loves all things spooky and mysterious, has written more than a dozen books for kids, including *Amazing Immortals*; *Terrible But True Awful Events in American History*; *True Hauntings: Deadly Disasters*; and *Spooky Cemeteries*, which wo a 2009 Children's Choice Book of the Year Award.